Original title:
The Ocean's Quiet Depths

Copyright © 2025 Creative Arts Management OÜ
All rights reserved.

Author: Micah Sterling
ISBN HARDBACK: 978-1-80587-448-5
ISBN PAPERBACK: 978-1-80587-918-3

Secrets of Serpentine Depths

Beneath the waves, a fish named Clyde,
Wore a top hat, which he took with pride.
He danced with a crab, both quite refined,
While jellyfish swayed, completely blind.

They threw a party in a coral hall,
Where seaweed snacks lined the glittering wall.
A shrimp DJ spun tunes with great flair,
While dolphins cheered, with fins in the air.

Rippling Stillness

In the shimmering hush, old turtles snore,
While plankton plot a dance on the floor.
They giggle and wiggle, all in a line,
Who knew such critters could move so fine?

A seahorse winks, with a wink that's sly,
As sea anemones simply sigh,
For being so still, they miss the beat,
While swimming along, the fish get a treat.

The Lure of the Briny Deep

A crab named Chip caught a whiff so sweet,
Of kelp-flavored popcorn on ocean's street.
He gathered his pals, it was time to feast,
On salty delights that would surely please.

But every time they tried to dive in,
A wave of laughter made it hard to begin.
With splashes and giggles, they were afloat,
The briny snack party turned into a boat!

Below the Surface

Bubbles rose up from a clam who spoke,
Telling tales of a fish that once wore a cloak.
With seaweed hats and scales that shine,
Those underwater legends are quite divine!

A pufferfish puffed, trying hard to boast,
But all he could do was to float like a ghost.
While all the sea stars laughed with delight,
A sea cucumber just rolled out of sight.

The Allure of Deep Blue

In waters deep where seahorses play,
A crab's dance takes my thoughts away.
I ask a fish, 'Do you get bored?'
He winked and said, 'I've got a hoard!'

The jellyfish is like a balloon,
Floating high, it sings a tune.
With every sway, it seems to boast,
'How many tentacles? Just coast to coast!'

Mysteries of the Silent Sea

Why does the octopus change its hue?
Is it shy, or just trying to woo?
The starfish grins with five-faced cheer,
I asked it if it has a career.

With bubbles popping like silly jokes,
The dolphin dances with a bunch of folks.
'Let's surf some waves!' it suddenly squeaks,
Everyone giggles, their laughter peaks!

Beneath the Calm Surface

A clam opens wide, it's quite a sight,
Searching for pearls – but they're not quite right!
'They look like gumdrops!' I tease with glee,
The clam just sighed, 'Stop picking on me!'

The seaweed sways with a floppy grace,
Two fish collide in a playful race.
'We're just in training for the big sea show!'
As a turtle tumbles, 'Can I join the flow?'

The Hidden Harmony

In the kelp forest, a party is set,
Where eels share jokes about their pet.
Bold seagulls swoop, shouting, 'Look me!'
The fish below are giggling with glee.

Crustaceans clink their shells so loud,
'We're the sound crew for this underwater crowd!'
As the sun sets, it glimmers and sways,
Who knew the deep could be this fun always?

Chasing the Light Below

Fish in tuxedos swim with flair,
Crabs dance wildly, without a care.
A jellyfish floats, glowing so bright,
Saying, "I'm just here for the nightly light!"

The seaweed waves, a green parade,
An octopus pranks with a twist of shade.
A sea star whispers jokes, oh so bold,
As a clam complains, "It's too cold, too cold!"

Shadows of the Deep Blue

Fishy friends in shades of blue,
Sharing secrets, quite a crew.
A grouper grins, with a silly face,
Says, "Don't forget to leave some space!"

A shrimp plays tag, a crab calls truce,
"Why are your claws so much bigger, moose?"
The mackerel chuckles, swimming by,
"An elephant in the sea? Oh my!"

Dreams Adrift

A sea turtle dreams of flying high,
With seagulls laughing as they pass by.
"I wish I could dive and wiggle in glee,
But I'm just a shell with nowhere to be!"

A dolphin dances with a playful leap,
"Time for a nap! You go count sheep!"
But the waves giggle, can't let him rest,
"Come, splash around! It's a water fest!"

From the Abyss with Love

A pufferfish blows up, puff, puff, cheer,
"Look at me, friends! I'm a beach ball here!"
But a sardine laughs, quite in gleeful shock,
"When the tide rolls in, will you deflate, or flop?"

A whale sends hugs wrapped in a bubble,
"Coming up for air, but it's quite the struggle!"
As currents swirl, fish giggle away,
"Let's make waves, then find time to play!"

Serenity in the Salt

Fish with sunglasses, quite a sight,
They swim in circles, feeling bright.
Coral reefs dance, they wiggle just right,
Underwater parties last all night.

A crab plays drums on a shell so grand,
Jellyfish join in with a graceful hand.
Seahorses twirl, forming a band,
While seaweed sways to the music so planned.

Lullabies of the Sea Bed

Starfish snore on sandy beds,
Their dreams filled with jelly and bread.
Tiny fish giggle, tickling their heads,
As seagulls chuckle, their feathers spread.

An octopus juggles, what a surprise!
With eight flailing arms, it catches our eyes.
Clams close shut, shushing the cries,
While hermit crabs race, oh how time flies!

The Calm Between Storms

A whale sings low, it's quite a tune,
Scaring away gulls, making them swoon.
The sea turtles surf, on waves they balloon,
While dolphins play leapfrog with a hot air balloon.

Shrimp hold a conference, discussing their fate,
"Who's stealing the shells, we can't wait!"
Clownfish argue, "It's not that great!"
As anemones giggle, saying, "Oh, just wait!"

Veils of Aquatic Silence

Under the surface, where few dare to go,
A crab weaves tales, stealing the show.
Clownfish burst out, flaunting their glow,
As sea cucumbers listen, plotting for dough.

A starry night brings a disco ball,
Angelfish dance, having a ball.
Sea urchins grumble, "We can't have it all!"
But the seaweed sways, celebrating the call!

Beneath the Nautilus Shell

In a spiral home, a snail takes a nap,
Avoiding the fish who'd love a quick slap.
Seaweed tickles, but he just grins wide,
Dreaming of seas where he can glide.

Jellyfish shimmy like they own the show,
While crabs wear tuxedos, putting on a flow.
The fish throw a party, lights splash and twirl,
But our nautilus snoozes, in his own little whirl.

Silken Shadows

The octopus dances with eight left feet,
Spinning in silence, not quite discreet.
A shy little shrimp understood the cue,
And joined in the fun, oh what a view!

Starfish applaud, they just can't help it,
As the bubbles rise, and they start to flip.
With every sway, the sea turns bright,
Who knew under waves, there'd be such a sight?

Sanctuary of the Aquatic Realm

A crab in the corner counts crabcakes to bake,
While clownfish giggle, making no mistake.
The seashells gossip, a clam's off stage,
Saying he's wise, he's turned quite the page.

Bubbles rise up as a shrimp tells a tale,
Of swimming in circles, devoid of fail.
In this vibrant arena, laughter's the sound,
Where fins flip and flounder, joy does abound.

Depths of Reflection

Deep down below, where the bubbles play,
A fish checks his mirror, 'Is that gray?'.
Seahorses laugh, they know how it goes,
In currents of truth, hilarity flows.

Anemones sway, tickling fish in a row,
As seagulls above, squawk, jostle and throw.
But down in the depths, all worries dissolve,
It's funny how mysteries happily evolve.

Beneath the Surface

Fish in tuxedos dance with glee,
They twirl and spin, as happy as can be.
A crab plays chess, he's quite the pro,
While seaweed wiggles, putting on a show.

Dolphins wear shades in the bright sunlight,
Making waves with every playful bite.
An octopus serves drinks, just look at him train,
With eight hands mixed up in a wobbly game!

Bubbles burst joyfully, laughter fills the air,
As a starfish tells jokes, too silly to bear.
The magic of the deep, both goofy and grand,
Is a jellyfish laughing, with wobbly hands.

So take a dive down past where we dwell,
In this silly wonderland where all critters gel.
With a flip and a splash, the fun never ends,
Beneath the surface, where the laughter blends.

Murmurs of the Deep

Whales sing carols, off-key but sweet,
A symphony played with each gentle beat.
Clams clap their shells like they're at a rave,
While a snail on a surfboard tries to be brave.

Seahorses gossip, they love to conspire,
Trading tall tales that never get tired.
With a wink and a nudge, they share all their dreams,
In a world full of bubbles and giggling streams.

A sponge writes a novel, quite candid and bold,
With tales of the ocean, both funny and old.
As squids paint murals with colors that pop,
Creating a gallery that just won't stop.

So come hear the whispers, the chuckles and roars,
In a place where the laughter bursts through the shores.
Beneath waves of humor, a hilarious veil,
In the whispers of water, where joy will prevail.

Tides of Stillness

Here in the stillness, the wonders unfold,
Where sea cucumbers shimmer like gold.
A pufferfish giggles, puffs up with pride,
While turtles in sunglasses take a cool ride.

Barnacles gossip, stuck tight to their rocks,
Swapping silly secrets, with laughter that knocks.
Anemones sway in a delicate dance,
While fish tell bad jokes, hoping for a chance.

Coral reefs chuckle, in colors so bright,
As lobsters play tag in the warm fading light.
The calm of the tide, a comedic delight,
Bringing humor to depths where shadows take flight.

The stillness is bustling, a spectacle grand,
In these tranquil waters, where laughter is planned.
With a splash and a giggle that ripples the scene,
In tides of stillness, all things get routine.

Shadows in the Tide

In the shadows of waves, where the silkiness hides,
A crab with a top hat pretends to be guides.
The shadow fish chuckle, in colors of gloom,
As seahorses whisper, "We're here for the zoom!"

Eel in a tux, winks at a friend,
Says, "Life is a party, let's never pretend!"
While anemones dance with their sway and their braids,
In games of hilarity, absurdity pervades.

A dolphin plays tricks, surfboards on fins,
While jellyfish juggle tiny sea pins.
The shadows are bustling, oh what a sight,
Where laughter erupts from the depths of the night.

So come take a peek in this merriment ride,
Where shadows have stories that tickle inside.
In bubbles of joy, the mirth does collide,
In the shadows of tides, let your laughter abide.

Submerged Dreams

Fish in tuxedos dance with glee,
A crab plays checkers, just for me.
Seashells gossip, quite absurd,
While octopuses write a word.

Bubbles float like soap in air,
Turtles play tag without a care.
Starfish are stars in a weird way,
They shine bright in the ocean's ballet.

Mermaids giggle at my plight,
I trip on seaweed, what a sight!
Dolphins do flips, giving me shade,
As jellyfish throw a grand parade.

So here I float, quite a mess,
In a sea of laughter, I confess.
With fishy friends and tales so tall,
I'm the king of this underwater hall!

Quietude of the Sea

Crabs wear sunglasses, looking cool,
As seahorses gather for a school.
Anemones sway, their dance so sweet,
While shells hold parties, oh what a treat!

A clam gives speeches, oh so grand,
With pearls of wisdom in its hand.
Starfish stargaze at the moon's glow,
Jellyfish rave, putting on a show.

Whales play tag in harmonized tunes,
While eels compete in fashion swoons.
Seasalt popcorn's the latest craze,
As sea cucumbers dance in a daze.

In this calm, my heart takes flight,
With giggles echoed in the night.
The deep blue has a side so spry,
In the cozy depths where jests fly high!

Hidden Harmonies

Underwater karaoke night arrives,
With fishy voices, oh how it thrives!
A shark's the judge, with quite a grin,
As bubble choirs begin to sing in.

Seashells harmonize with great delight,
While squids play tambourines so bright.
A crab in a bowtie steals the show,
As dolphins dance in a sparkling flow.

Starfish clap with their five-armed charm,
As octopus juggles without alarm.
With each note, the sea sways along,
In these hidden harmonies, we belong.

So laugh along in the deep sea's cheer,
With fishy jokes echoing near.
This underwater concert brings such fun,
Creating memories 'til the day is done!

Beneath a Blanket of Blue

Under a quilt of marine surprise,
Seahorses wear the silliest ties.
A walrus relaxes with a wink,
While clams sip smoothies and think.

An octopus is a master chef,
Whipping up dishes, stealing the heft.
With gooey goo as the secret spice,
Creating flavors that are so nice.

Beneath the waves, I take a dive,
Where jellyfish play the coolest jive.
Turtles roll over, having a ball,
It's an underwater carnival.

So, join the fun beneath the waves,
Where laughter bubbles and mischief braves.
In this blue paradise, all is bright,
With salty smiles, it's pure delight!

Tranquil Depths

In a realm where fish wear hats,
Bubbles talk and dance like brats.
Seaweed sways in a goofy groove,
Even crabs have made a move.

Turtles race in slow-motion bliss,
Sharks are dentists, that's their business.
Starfish throw a disco ball,
While dolphins giggle, having a ball.

Octopuses juggle with great flair,
Clams are gossiping without a care.
Jellyfish float like drunk balloons,
Making waves with their funny tunes.

The depths are silly, that's the truth,
Where every wave holds a dose of youth.
In this watery world, laughter flows,
Turning serious times into silly shows.

Underwater Reveries

Seahorses ride on bubbles bright,
Belly flops are quite the sight.
Fish with sunglasses glide through waves,
Plotting mischief, oh, how it saves!

Whales hum tunes with a bass so deep,
While clams snore softly, lost in sleep.
Crabs crack jokes with a pinch of sass,
In the depths, they're all quite brash.

Eels tell tales, all tangled in fun,
Lights flicker like a playful pun.
Mermaids laugh, with hair all frizzy,
Waves carrying giggles, oh so dizzy.

In this strange underwater dream,
Even plankton join the crafty scheme.
Each flick of a fin, each splashy laugh,
Makes the deep a silly photograph.

Mirage of the Deep

A fish wearing shoes is on parade,
While sea cucumbers serenade.
Bubble parties hosted by clowns,
Float away all the frowns.

Anemones dance in the current so free,
Sea spiders weave webs of comedy.
Lobsters riddle like jesters bold,
While treasures hide their stories untold.

The water shimmers with jokes galore,
Barnacles laugh as the tides explore.
Crab comedians on coral stages,
Make the depths lively through ages.

With each wave, a chuckle is brewed,
In the bizarre depths, don't misconstrue.
Under the surface, nobody's gray,
Just a world where laughter holds sway.

Cradle of the Tide

Tadpoles trade gossip with a glee,
Fish crack up like they're on TV.
Diving deep through waters clear,
Every splash brings forth a cheer.

Squids pulling pranks with ink so vast,
Ticklish turtles laugh as they pass.
Barnacles sing in perfect pitch,
To a tune that gets the sea to twitch.

Starfish toss wishes to the sky,
While seahorses think they can fly.
Deep in the blue, joy multiplies,
Life's a laugh, no need for sighs.

As currents swirl with humor bright,
This underwater world is pure delight.
In the cradle where the tide rolls wide,
Funny creatures enjoy the ride.

In the Heart of the Deep

Bubbles rise with a pop,
Like secrets that won't stop.
Fish wear ties made of kelp,
Laughing at what they've dealt.

Crabs do the cha-cha slide,
Shells acting as their guide.
Clams tell jokes with a grin,
Shells clapping in the din.

An octopus paints each wall,
While sea turtles have a ball.
Jellyfish float like balloons,
Dancing to their own tunes.

Explorers dive down to play,
Surfing on each playful wave.
Mermaids sing with a twist,
Join in, you won't want to miss!

Layers of Silence Below

Quiet layers, what a tease,
Whispers carried by a breeze.
Anemones are having fun,
Hiding from the golden sun.

Starfish are experts at chill,
Relaxed on the ocean's sill.
They wink with their little arms,
Crafty with all of their charms.

Turtles don sombreros bright,
Passing by with all their might.
They laugh at the silly fish,
Who boast of their latest dish.

Down below the moonlight dances,
Creatures join in their own prances.
A concert in the depths unfolds,
Where the sea spins tales so bold!

Whispers Beneath the Surface

In the depths, thoughts travel far,
Fish hold meetings like a czar.
Sardines gossip, tattle-tale,
While eels glide without a sail.

Underneath the rippling sea,
Crabs recite poetry with glee.
Seaweed swings in vibrant hues,
While dolphins sing their ocean blues.

The sand's a blanket, soft and sweet,
Where starfish throw a dance-off meet.
Checkered shells as their prizes shine,
The winner's cheer is quite divine.

In this world of funny sights,
Creatures sparkle with pure delights.
Down below, let laughter ring,
Bursting bubbles are the thing!

Abyssal Serenity

Peering deep where shadows play,
Seahorses trot in a grand ballet.
They nudge each other with flair,
While sea cucumbers just stare.

A grouper tells his fishy tales,
Of treasures found in sunlit gales.
Crabs roll their eyes at the intent,
Sipping sea water with a content.

Every bubble holds a joke,
As a whale plays a smoky croak.
The rays spin in joyous leaps,
While the barnacles count their sheep.

Creatures of all shapes parade,
In the coolness, not a charade.
Underneath the surface blue,
Funny things, they just pursue!

The Horizon's Embrace

Waves whisper secrets, a clam in disguise,
A fish with a mustache, oh how it belies!
Seagulls are gossiping, squawking with cheer,
While crabs play charades in the sand without fear.

The sun dances lightly on water so grand,
As jellyfish waltz, they glide and they stand.
A starfish takes selfies, with shells in its clutch,
While barnacles giggle, they're having too much!

Turtles in sunglasses, looking so cool,
Waves rolling in, we're breaking that rule.
The horizon calls out with a cheeky loud tone,
"Swim with a dolphin, but don't be alone!"

With each silly splash, we can't help but feel,
The joy of the sea is a truly great deal.
So let's raise our glasses, to this watery jest,
For laughter's the treasure, the ocean's the quest!

Melodies of the Mysterious Deep

Bubbles burst laughter from fish in a band,
A clam on a sax, now isn't that grand?
Octopuses juggling, put on quite the show,
While sea turtles go disco, putting on quite a flow.

The seaweed's a curtain for the sea's grand ballet,
With dolphins performing, they splash and they sway.
A crab with a headset, he's tuning the beat,
While starfish play maracas, oh isn't that neat?

Herring sing harmony, fish swim in time,
Anemones clapping, they're feeling sublime.
Shells are the audience, all lined up to cheer,
As pearls drop some puns, tickling all with cheer.

As waves keep on crashing, a chorus rings clear,
With giggles and splashes, we hold nothing dear.
So join in the laughter, let's dive to the deep,
Where melodies linger, and secrets we keep!

Echoing Silence

Under the surface, it's quiet and shy,
Except for a whale, with a hiccuping sigh.
Giant squid reading, with a monocle tight,
While turtles tell tales in the softest moonlight.

Bubblegum bubbles, they giggle and pop,
As lobsters in tuxedos decide they won't stop.
An octopus whispers, with ink in his pen,
Writing postcards to sailors, oh where have they been?

The silence is golden, or maybe it's blue,
As fish crack some jokes, that are way overdue.
A clam rolls its eyes at the antics, oh lord!
And seahorses giggling, send laughter abroad!

In depths of the quiet, humor finds its way,
Renting out space for a fish cabaret.
So dive into laughter, let's share in the fun,
For echoing silence is never outdone!

Labyrinths of Aquamarine

Through twisting passages of wavy delight,
A shrimp sings a tune, under moon's glowing light.
The coral like castles, don't be shy to roam,
Just watch for the turtles, they're calling it home.

A grouper with glasses, so wise and so grand,
Gives nuggets of wisdom, for fish in the land.
The eels tell tall tales, twisting paths of fun,
While sea cucumbers join in, all having a run.

A treasure map written in bubbles and glee,
Points to the spot where all fish claim to be.
With giddy excitement, they spin in a whirl,
Flowing past seashells, each one is a pearl.

So wander the maze filled with laughter and cheer,
The depths keep on tickling for all who draw near.
In labyrinths of laughter, adventure awaits,
Just follow the giggles, for joy it creates!

Beneath the Glittering Tide

Bubbles rise like little boats,
Fish wear hats and swim with coats.
Crabs do the moonwalk on soft sand,
Seahorses dance, oh so unplanned.

Whales hum tunes from olden days,
They have karaoke nights and play.
Anemones throw a wild ball,
Jellyfish slide and have a sprawl.

Starfish gossip in ocean's glow,
Octopus sketches, putting on a show.
Clownfish invite all for a snack,
Waving their fins, "Hey, don't you slack!"

Under waves, the fun's alive,
Creatures twirl, strive to outlive.
In the deep, they laugh and glide,
A community of joy, far and wide.

Secrets of Distant Shores

Shells whisper tales of treasure maps,
Crabs sell cookies, "Get your snaps!"
Turtles roll dice and bet on snails,
Seagulls swoop low with their fancy pails.

Seashells gossip about the past,
"Did you see that wave? Wow, what a blast!"
Mermaids compose an ocean song,
While dolphins debate if it's right or wrong.

Fishes play tag, darting about,
"Catch me if you can!" they shout.
Corals share stories from days gone by,
And starfish laugh with a winked eye.

On the shore, they toss and sway,
Gathering secrets, come what may.
Life is a part where the tide won't end,
It's all in fun, my ocean friend.

The Stillness Below

Deep under where the sunlight fades,
Fish wear tuxedos, throw parades.
Crabs are the judges in a dance-off,
With every shuffle, they laugh and scoff.

Giant squids win with an inky flair,
While clownfish chuckle, waving with care.
Cone snails host trivia on the sea floor,
"Did you know what's behind that door?"

Octopus chefs whip up a meal,
With a pinch of seaweed and spin of eel.
They serve it fresh on a barnacle plate,
"Bon appétit! There's no time to wait!"

Comics on shells with puns to unfold,
Jokes of the deep that never get old.
In the calm, where laughter swells,
You'll find the humor in oceanic wells.

Oceanic Secrets Untold

Blubbery seals in a whirlpool spin,
Jellyfish giggle, "Where do we begin?"
Tides have tickled their funny bones,
With foam that dances on eight-legged cones.

Sea urchins wear sunglasses and chill,
Sipping on seaweed, it's quite a thrill.
Guppies tell tales of the great abyss,
While playing tag in a watery mist.

Mysterious shadows swim near the light,
"Is it a shark, or just a kite?"
Eels sing songs that bubble and pop,
Inviting all to dance till they drop.

In the depths where giggles reside,
Creatures of humor, side by side.
With every ripple and wave that holds,
There's laughter in every secret it folds.

Depths Unseen

In the waters way down low,
Fish play hide and seek with woe.
Octopus wearing a hat quite tall,
Says, "Welcome to my underwater ball!"

Crabs dance sideways with great delight,
While squids ink secrets in the night.
A turtle sings a slothful tune,
With dolphins twirling beneath the moon.

Shimmering jellyfish wave goodbye,
As sea cucumbers just sit and sigh.
Anemones tickle passing fish,
While sea stars dream of their next big wish!

In this realm of moans and gleeful shouts,
You'll find the funniest of sea routes.
Mermaids giggle in a bubble bath,
While the seaweed groans in a math class.

The Stillness Below

A clam with a shell can't quite shut,
Cracks jokes under a coral hut.
Seahorses prance in a tiny race,
While starfish giggle in their fixed place.

Bubbles rise with each laugh and cheer,
Even the seashells lend an ear.
A whale nearby sings out in jest,
Hoping to win the shellfish best!

Pufferfish puff up just for fun,
Claiming they're the only one.
With a wink and a swim, they boast and bray,
"Who needs a beach? We're here to stay!"

As the tide comes in and out with grace,
The gills all giggle in their fishy space.
With seaweed raves and plankton cheer,
Life's a party down here, my dear!

Voices of the Waves

The waves crash in, a comedic scene,
Where sea slugs do a wiggly routine.
Fishes gossip in bubbles, oh so loud,
While a crab takes selfies, feeling proud.

Blowfish boasting with cheeks all round,
Claim they're the kings of the colorful sound.
An eel jests, "I'm just here to shock,"
As kelp strands giggle on the dock.

The barnacles whisper secrets of lore,
About treasures lost and ships of yore.
Lobsters laugh in their crusty attire,
While sea turtles join in with a choir.

Laughter echoes in the salty air,
As waves dance by without a care.
Join the bubble party, it's quite a craze,
In this hilarious world where life always plays!

Veiled Currents

Under hues of blue and green tide,
Silly fish shuffle, unable to hide.
A swordfish fencing with seaweed foes,
While a clownfish tells jokes that nobody knows.

An octopus twirls with eight left feet,
Trying to dance, but facing defeat.
Crustaceans throw a dance party tonight,
With shrimp DJ spinning tunes just right.

The deep is alive with giggles and grins,
As nature's quirks become our sins.
The playful currents sway to a beat,
With ticklish tides, life feels so sweet!

There's laughter in the bubbles that rise,
Under the surface, beneath the skies.
Join us down where the silly play,
In the currents' veiled and whimsical way!

Dreams in the Coral Reef

In bright coral beds, fish dance on cue,
With fins flapping wildly, they're quite the crew.
A seahorse in slippers, just chillin' with flair,
Sipping on seaweed, not a single care.

A turtle in shades, on a beach he does lay,
Baking in sunlight, enjoying the day.
His buddies all gawk, as they splash and they dive,
Laughing at how he just won't come alive.

The crabs hold a party, with shells on their feet,
Playing the conch, it's a real tasty treat.
They've invited a shrimp, who'll dance on a dime,
Showing off moves, they've perfected with time.

With bubbles and giggles, the fish sing along,
To the tune of the tides, they all join in song.
For laughter runs deep, in the shimmering sea,
Where every wave whispers, "Just let it be!"

Underwater Reverie

In a castle of kelp, where the gurgles abound,
A flounder plays chess on a soft sandy mound.
A pufferfish pouts, with his spiky hairdo,
While dolphins discuss who can jump through the blue.

The jellyfish waltz, with the rhythm of tide,
As octopuses juggle, their skills can't be denied.
With ink-squirting laughs, they turn slick on a dime,
Creating a ruckus—oh, isn't it prime?

The seahorses giggle, all tucked in a nook,
Reading the latest in "Fishy Storybook."
With a splash of a fin, they leap in delight,
In this quirky realm where the world's ever bright.

As bubbles rise gently, a treasure to find,
A sponge with a smile and a very good rhyme.
For laughter's the pearl in this watery grace,
Every nook has a tale, every wave a warm embrace.

Tranquil Waters Lurk

Where the sand meets the sea, a crab jokes in glee,
With a pinch and a wink, oh so cheekily free.
He whispers to fish, "Have you heard of the fluke?
He slipped on a conch shell and danced like a kook!"

In currents that giggle, a dolphin appears,
Singing sweet ballads that tickle your ears.
But a grouchy old eel, twirls his tail with disdain,
Says, "Stop all this nonsense, it drives me insane!"

Beneath waves so calm, a party does brew,
A clam and a shrimp have a joke or two.
With bubbles as confetti, the merriment flows,
Tickling the seaweed, as laughter just grows.

As fish flaunt their colors and sea stars all twirl,
Life's like a dance in this whimsical whirl.
So plunge in the fun, let your worries all drift,
For beneath gentle waves lies the ocean's true gift!

The Depths' Embrace

In the cozy abyss, where the glowworms all wink,
A lobster in glasses takes time out to think.
"Why did the clam rush?" he muses with flair,
"Because it was shell-shocked, too much to bear!"

A catfish with glasses reads books on the reef,
While starfish play poker, disguising their grief.
With a wink and a nudge, the pufferfish pouts,
"Raise the stakes, my friends, let's see what this's about!"

As currents keep swirling, a mermaid does hum,
Creating sweet waves with her delightful strum.
A giggle erupts, when the shrimp bursts a bubble,
With laughter and joy, they all dodge the trouble.

So here in the depths, where the funny fish flit,
Life's a tangled web, and every twist is a hit.
In silty embraces, they gather and cheer,
For laughter's the treasure that keeps them all near!

Elysium of the Blue

In the sea, a fish wears a tie,
Thought he'd look sharp, oh me, oh my.
But the crabs just laughed, in a shellfish cheer,
Fashion advice? Don't ask, my dear.

Jellyfish dance with a neon glow,
Wobbling along, putting on a show.
A sea turtle giggles, what a sight,
Paddle faster, oh what a fright!

The seahorse struts like it's on a catwalk,
While the octopus plays a game of rock.
"Check out my ink!" it says with glee,
But it spills out instead on a passing sea bee.

In the blue, there's laughter all around,
With mermaids spinning in the calm, profound.
Who knew the sea could be so silly?
Splashes of joy, a giggling filly.

Secrets of the Marine Softness

A starfish wonders about the stars,
"Are they just ocean critters with fancy cars?"
The seahorse chuckles, nudging its mate,
"Those twinkling fish must be quite late!"

Coral sings along to a whale's tune,
Swaying gently, morning to noon.
"Hey, are we having a bubble bath?"
"Nah, just the usual, silliness math."

Anemones wave like disco balls,
"Come dance with us!" they joyfully call.
While clowns, with their joyful faces,
Do flips and twirls in playful graces.

Down below, the sea floor's a stage,
Fishy performers, bursting with rage.
Why take life serious? They wink, they nod,
In the marine soft world, they'll have a applaud!

Fathoms of Solitude

In the deep, a hermit crab's sad,
Lost its shell, oh isn't that bad?
He tries on a can, a bottle, a shoe,
"Fashion is tough, but I'll make do!"

A grouper sighs, watching this plight,
"Fashion advice? Just frightful sight!"
While starfish giggle, all in good cheer,
"Hey, just be you, we all steer clear!"

An octopus dreams of a big fat pearl,
"Wanna trade?" he suggests with a twirl.
But the clam just clams up, too shy to show,
"Keep your treasures, I'm good, you know!"

So down in the dark, they all ride the wave,
In a world of jests, so fun and brave.
Solitude's not dreary, it's a giggle spree,
In the shadows, they dance their sea jubilee.

Beneath the Waves' Whisper

Bubbles tickle fish as they glide,
"Who's the fastest? Let's take a ride!"
A pufferfish puffs, "I'm the champ!"
But a little sardine zips right by, like a lamp!

Giant squids contemplate life's lore,
"Is there more than just ink to explore?"
While a crab rolls his eyes, looking bored,
"Get real, my friend, stop being ignored!"

Octopus joins the underwater race,
"Watch me jet!" it shouts with grace.
But alas, it trips over a lost shoe,
And giggles erupt at the slip, it's true!

So deep down below, where whispers play,
Fish flop and flop till the end of the day.
In watery laughter, they find their bliss,
Beneath the waves, it's pure comic mist.

Beneath the Coral Canopy

In a reef where fish love to dance,
A clownfish tried to impress a prance.
Said to a crab in a shell so tight,
"Do you think my fins are just too bright?"

A starfish laughed, he had five arms,
Claimed he could woo with his many charms.
But all his moves were a tad too slow,
And the parrotfish stole the show!

The sea turtle, wise, shook his head,
"Oh, dear friends, you're not quite fed!"
They ordered sushi, but it was fishy,
A strange meal that made them all quite sissy!

So they danced and laughed 'neath colors so bold,
In the coral, stories of friendship unfold.
A lesson learned beneath waves so swell:
When you're with friends, all is well!

Where Shadows Dwell

In twilight's grip, the eel does glide,
With a grin that most would hide.
He winked at a grouper, small and round,
"Why so shy? Let's dance, profound!"

A hermit crab scurried, fast and spry,
Challenged the eel, "Don't be shy!"
But in a swirl, he slipped and fell,
In a dance-off with no one to tell!

An octopus giggled, with colors to show,
"When I'm in a jam, I just let it go!"
He mimicked their moves in a slippery way,
And everyone laughed till the break of day.

So in shadows they pranced, a whimsical sight,
In the depths, they spun in sheer delight.
Monsters of laughter, not fear to dwell,
Where shadows brighten and friendships swell!

Lullabies of the Abyss

Down in the dark, a lullaby sang,
A squid played tunes with a twinkling tang.
A whale joined in with a deep, loud note,
But the little shrimp just floated and wrote.

"Why's he so big and I'm so small?"
Said a tiny fish with a question for all.
"It's all about the volume you bring,"
Said the clam with a shell that could swing!

They took a bet on who could sing best,
But a puffed-up puffer just won the test.
With bubbles flying and voices so dear,
They filled the abyss with musical cheer!

So they crooned through the currents, an elegant mess,
With laughter echoing, none felt the stress.
In the deep, they found tunes they wouldn't suppress,
Singing soft lullabies of sheer happiness!

Moonlit Ripples

Under moonlit ripples, a seal took a dive,
Declared he was king of the fishy hive!
The dolphins just chuckled, flipped in their grace,
"Let's have a party, come join the race!"

The krill danced in lines, they spun and they swayed,
As the seal sang loudly and slightly delayed.
"With friends all around, we laugh till we cry,
Unless there's a shark, then we're all very shy!"

But as shadows bloomed in the shimmering light,
A jellyfish glided, so fluid and bright.
"You call that a race? I float like a dream!"
The turtles all cheered, "Join in, it's a theme!"

So they twirled and they twinkled till dawn brought a glow,
In waters that giggled, with currents that flow.
Moonlit reflections, a fun little trip,
The sea's just a place where the wild come equipped!

Secrets of the Blue

Bubbles rise like giggles loud,
As fish dance beneath a blanket shroud.
They hide their jokes in coral caves,
While starfish snicker at the waves.

An octopus plays hide-and-seek,
With squids that wiggle, oh so sleek.
They tickle the urchins, who roll and pout,
In a world where laughter is all about.

A pirate ship sails with a crew of clowns,
Throwing fish snacks to the towns.
They laugh as they trip on barnacle stones,
Creating a ruckus in aquatic tones.

So if you dive and take a peek,
You'll find the sea is far from bleak.
With secrets tangled in seaweed knots,
Prepare for fun in watery spots.

Tides of Tranquility

A turtle snoozes on a floating log,
Dreaming of marshmallows and a dancing frog.
Crabs play chess with shells from the shore,
While dolphins giggle, wanting more.

Seagulls squawk about the latest craze,
In a fashion show with fish in a daze.
They strut and show in their feathery coats,
While the deep blue chuckles at their funny quotes.

When waves come in with a splash and a roar,
It's the jellyfish throwing a dance on the floor.
Their disco lights twinkle in the night,
With creatures swaying, oh what a sight!

As the tide turns with a jovial fling,
The sea learns how to laugh and to sing.
Calm down, dear waves, it's all in good fun,
Under the bright, spinning golden sun.

Veils of the Deep

A clownfish wears a tiny hat,
While a great big whale just sits and chats.
They tell tall tales of finding socks,
Amongst the shells and wandering rocks.

Anemones sway as if to dance,
While jellyfish float in a comical trance.
With each little shimmer and wiggly sway,
They gossip and giggle the entire day.

The seabed's a stage for fishy plays,
Where eels create drama in twisted ways.
They get tangled up in a mess of fun,
While everyone's laughing under the sun.

If you dive deeper, don't be afraid,
Join the party that nature's made.
The veils hide laughter, but look close and see,
There's joy in the depths, wild and free.

Echoes of Silent Waters

In the hush of the blue, secrets ring clear,
As a fish tells a joke that only you hear.
A crab with a mustache struts real proud,
While shrimp form a conga line, oh so loud.

Buoyant bubbles carry whispers of glee,
A surfboard for seals, just wait and see.
They try to surf on a giant wave,
End up splashing and laughing, oh how they rave.

A treasure chest dancing with broken dreams,
Full of lost socks and shiny beams.
Mermaids giggle as they share their finds,
Joking all day with playful minds.

So down in the depths, just listen and laugh,
The quiet below is a comedic half.
In echoes of silence, the sea's punchline waits,
With splashes of humor at all its gates.

Depths of the Heart

A fish with glasses, oh so wise,
It taught the crabs to wear a tie.
They'd dance on waves, a silly sight,
While seaweed clapped in sheer delight.

The starfish giggled, tickled pink,
As bubbles floated, life in sync.
A dolphin juggled with a shell,
And all the sea critters laughed so well.

With octopus arms waving high,
He tried to wave, but oh my, my!
Slipping on eels, he took a dive,
Then jumped back up, feeling alive!

So deep below where currents play,
The laughter echoes, night and day.
In every ripple, a joke is found,
Among the waves, joy does abound.

Odes to the Quiet Waters

A clam with dreams, oh what a sight,
Hoped to be a pearl in moonlight.
But he just lay there, snoozing still,
While shrimp performed a tap dance drill.

An otter slipped and lost his shell,
With a splash and dash, he rang the bell.
He flipped and flopped, a wild routine,
All for the crowd, a seaweed queen.

The turtles rolled their eyes and sighed,
As fishy tales and puns abide.
Sardines swam past, all in a row,
Chasing the giggles, putting on a show.

In the stillness, secrets creep,
With catchy rhymes that make us leap.
For laughter flows, a current bright,
In the quiet waters, pure delight.

The Dance of the Deep

With bubbles popping like champagne,
The fish all gathered for the fun.
They spun around in a grand ballet,
As sea cucumbers cheered, 'Well done!'

Anemones waved in the gentle tide,
While sea horses tap danced side by side.
The jellyfish glowed in a light parade,
But they didn't mind, they love the shade.

The blowfish puffed, all big and round,
Trying to dance without a sound.
But tripped on a rock, what a sight!
And all the sea chortled with delight.

So come and swirl in the deep blue bay,
Where fins and giggles steal the day.
A festival of bubbles and cheers,
As laughter echoes through the years.

Still Waters Run Deep

In still waters where the minnows play,
A frog croaks jokes in a funny way.
He leaps and lands on a lily pad,
While turtles grin, they like the lad.

The otters slide with giggles galore,
Hoping for more, they beg for a score.
A walrus joins in, with a hearty laugh,
As fish waltz by, taking their path.

The crickets chirp a quirky beat,
While gorging on snacks, they find it neat.
Drifting down in a current warm,
The puns afloat, they break the norm.

So let's enjoy the tides so sweet,
Where nature's humor makes life complete.
For in the depths, there's fun galore,
Just dive on in, let's all explore!

Ripples of Redemption

In a floating chair, a fish took a seat,
Wearing sunglasses, oh what a treat!
He sipped on seaweed, with a grin so wide,
Said he'd surf the waves, but ran out of tide.

A crab in a tux, danced on the sand,
With slick moves that surely were poorly planned.
He stumbled and tumbled, made quite the scene,
Even the starfish laughed; oh, how they were keen!

A dolphin swam by, with a boombox in tow,
Blaring pop tunes, making fish want to flow.
They formed a conga line, in not-so-straight rows,
But the jellyfish joined, and chaos arose!

In this splashy ballet, they jived with delight,
As the turtles looked on, holding back their fright.
With each little ripple, they shared a good cheer,
The punchline was clear: the fun's always here!

Calm in the Undersea

A walrus in slippers had quite the stride,
He'd waddle to nowhere, like a surprising guide.
With a twirl and a twist, he slipped on a pearl,
Declaring, 'This is my dance!' in a slow, silly whirl.

A sea cucumber chuckled as fish swam on by,
'In this bed of green socks, I could surely fly!'
The truth of the matter, we all understood,
When the seaweed tickled, it was time to be good.

A turtle named Gary thought he'd try to race,
But naps were his forte, not a fast-paced chase.
He snoozed on a rock, with dreams of the sky,
While the crabs took selfies, giggling nearby.

So in this soft haven, under currents and waves,
Where laughter and silliness swim like brave knaves,
The creatures found joy in the silliest ways,
Disguised in the calm of those blue watery bays.

Cascades of Stillness

A fish wearing glasses was reading the news,
He said, 'Flounder found fortune, now that's some good views!'
While a pufferfish giggled, inflating with pride,
Said, 'In this quiet world, I am queen of the tide!'

A mollusk was grumpy, all closed in his shell,
'It's too quiet here, can you find me a bell?'
But the clownfish just hummed, with a skip in his fin,
'Shells are to rest in; come play, don't give in!'

A sea anemone tried stand-up, oh dear,
Telling sea jokes while the fish tanked the cheer.
With one punchline in hand, a giant wave crashed,
And everyone giggled at how it all splashed.

In this whimsical calm, where the waves softly sigh,
Where laughter bubbles up, and the seahorses fly,
The stillness was vibrant, alive and so bright,
Making waves of laughter stretch into the night!

Shallows of Serenity

In the shallows, the flounder tried yoga one day,
While the seahorses watched, saying, 'Hey, look, hooray!'

But the barnacles laughed as he toppled with grace,
And the whole fishy crew fell into his space!

A clam thought he'd sing in a low, croaking key,
But the squids rolled their eyes, 'Oh, clam, let it be!'
'With those vocal chords, you'd scare off a crab,
We'd rather hear bubbles than that sandy drab.'

A starfish performed, giving all that he could,
Flip after flip, like a sea-style neighborhood.
But his final bow put him face-first in the muck,
And the nearby seaweed—oh boy, what bad luck!

Yet in these shallows, under sun's friendly rays,
The fish found great comfort in their splashy displays.
With giggles and joy, through the sands they would dance,

In the humor of home, they'd sing and they'd prance!

Hidden Currents

Beneath the waves, a fish once cried,
"I lost my lunch, my pride, my guide!"
A crab just chuckled, with a wink,
"Just keep swimming; don't overthink!"

A dolphin danced, with playful flips,
While seahorses rehearsed their scripts.
They'd put on shows for passing stars,
And ride the tides like fancy cars.

An octopus was king of tricks,
He'd squirt some ink, then vanish quick.
"I'm here, I'm there!" he loved to boast,
But really, he just liked to coast!

The jellyfish, with stings so mild,
Said, "Bring your friends, I'm fun, not wild!"
They floated by, a sneaky crew,
And giggled softly, just like you.

Reflections in Aquamarine

A turtle wore a pair of shades,
Said, "I'm on break! Just catching rays!"
He flopped back down with such great grace,
While others raced, he found his place.

A clownfish told a silly joke,
He said, "I'm funny—no, no coked!"
The corals laughed, they swayed with glee,
And bubbles popped like laughter's spree.

A starfish shaped like Donald Duck,
Claimed he was lucky, or out of luck!
He posed and grinned, a goofy sight,
While seaweed danced, so wild and bright.

Anemones joined with every sway,
In colorful skirts, they'd twirl and play.
In depths so blue, such fun they'd find,
Where shadows whispered, spirits unwind.

Journey to the Silent Depths

In seas so deep, where echoes play,
A fishy voice came out to say,
"What's that smell? Did someone stew?"
A whale replied, "Not me, it's you!"

They traveled far on jelly ships,
Where squid had picnics, sharing chips.
With guffaws that shook the seaweed beds,
They gathered all their fishy heads.

A voyage planned beneath the tide,
Where sea turtles swam with starry pride.
They mapped the treasure, fun to seek,
But found just socks and one lost shoe peak!

"Who needs gold, when we've got laughs?"
Said one lone shrimp among the gaffs.
With every wave, they'd glide and slide,
Making memories with laughter tied.

The Caves of Forgetfulness

In caves so dark, a lobster snored,
Dreaming of all the snacks he hoarded.
He woke with a start, said, "What's the fuss?"
Then forgot it all, with a little rust.

A clownfish painted on the wall,
In polka dots, he had a ball.
"I'm an artist!" he proudly claimed,
But underwater, he went unnamed.

Echoes bounced like laughter's cheer,
While shrimp danced like they had no fear.
"Let's throw a party!" they all agreed,
But one forgot who was in the lead.

With bubbles rising in sheer delight,
They played hide-and-seek 'til the night.
And as they laughed in their little zone,
They created joy in the sea, their home.

Whispers Beneath the Waves

The fish gossip, making a fuss,
While turtles giggle and create a fuss.
Seaweed dances like it's got no care,
And crabs snicker in their sandy lair.

Starfish throw parties, oh what a sight,
With bubbles and shells; they party all night.
Seahorses twirl in a whimsical waltz,
While dolphins make jokes about fishy faults.

A clam's got a secret, but it's quite shy,
Says pearls are overrated, oh me, oh my!
Octopuses juggle, what a sight to see,
Their eight arms waving, full of glee!

So let's dive in, to this world so bright,
Where laughter echoes, and fish take flight.
In this watery wonder, come have some fun,
Join in the laughter, there's joy for everyone!

Secrets of the Abyss

In the deep, the secrets swim around,
Fish tell tall tales from where they are found.
A squid plays hide and seek, what a tease,
With its friend the ray, they dart with such ease.

Crabs boast of battles, their claws held high,
While lobsters gossip as they pass by.
Anemones chuckle at passing young men,
"Does he know he's wearing a seaweed pen?"

A pufferfish swells up, it's not what you think,
"Honestly, it's just to make some kids blink!"
With jellyfish prancing like they missed the cue,
They say, "Swim on in, we'll show you the view!"

In the abyss where the light rarely peeks,
Comes laughter and fun, so loud it speaks.
So plunge into waters, and do not be shy,
This deep blue world has a wink and a sigh!

Echoes in the Blue

Bubbles ripple with a giggle and cheer,
As sea turtles whisper, "Come join us here!"
Fish flash their scales with a wink and a swirl,
And laughter erupts in this underwater whirl.

An octopus mimics, oh what a tool,
"Look at me dance, I'm the king of the pool!"
The clownfish chuckles with stripes all aglow,
"Why did the coral get kicked out of the show?"

A sea captain crab, wearing a hat,
Boasts to the fish how it's close to the mat.
"Throw me a line, I'll tie it with flair,
For treasures and trinkets, I just do not care!"

So join in the echoes so merry and bright,
For the creatures below are a glorious sight.
In the blue where the chuckles make ripples of glee,
Let's dance with the dolphins, come swim along with me!

Depths of Solitude

In silent depths, a lonely whale stares,
Wonders if anyone else really cares.
With a bubble and sigh, it sings a soft tune,
While the sea cucumbers just snooze until noon.

A lonely anemone sways with a sigh,
"I'm here all alone, but why should I cry?"
The rocks whisper back with an echoing cheer,
"Embrace your own quiet, have none of that fear!"

Down in the depth, where the sun rarely glows,
Lives a hermit crab, with nowhere to go.
"Might as well rave in this shell I call home,
Oh wait, now I'm stuck, guess I'll just moan!"

But even in solitude, there's laughter at play,
For the sea life finds joy in a humorous way.
So next time you ponder the depths all alone,
Remember the giggles beneath the sea's tone!

www.ingramcontent.com/pod-product-compliance
Lightning Source LLC
Chambersburg PA
CBHW060145230426
43661CB00003B/572